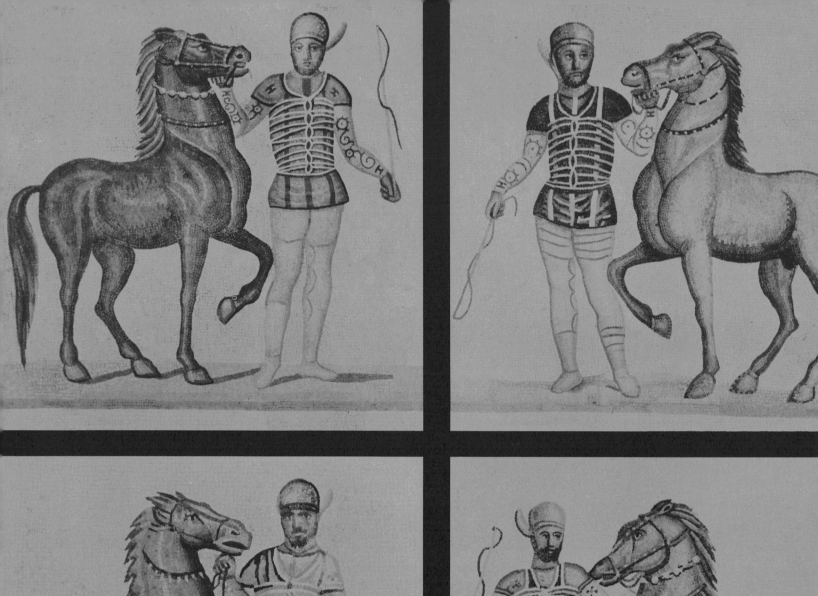

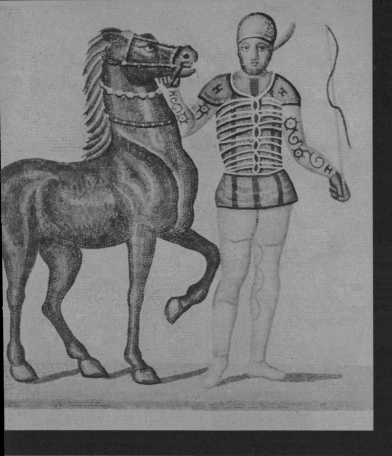

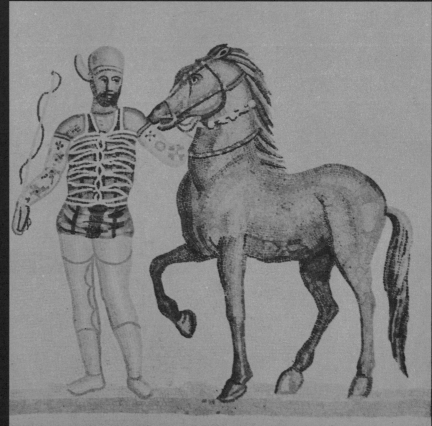

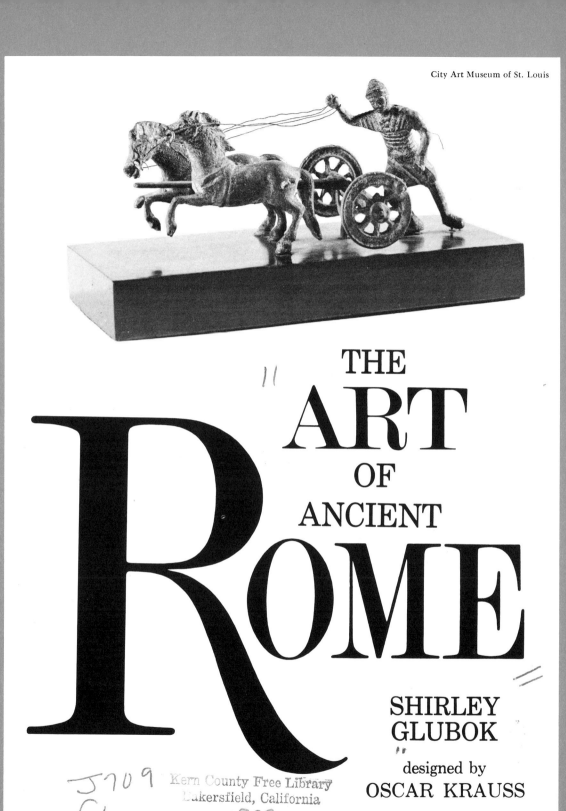

THE
ART
OF
ANCIENT
ROME

**SHIRLEY
GLUBOK**

designed by
OSCAR KRAUSS

HARPER & ROW, PUBLISHERS • NEW YORK, EVANSTON, AND LONDON

THE AUTHOR GRATEFULLY ACKNOWLEDGES THE ASSISTANCE OF:

OTTO J. BRENDEL, Professor of Art History and Archaeology, Columbia University

MARGARET R. SCHERER, Former Research Associate, The Metropolitan Museum of Art

MASTER MARK FRIEDMAN

•

Other Books By SHIRLEY GLUBOK:

THE ART OF ANCIENT EGYPT
THE ART OF LANDS IN THE BIBLE
THE ART OF ANCIENT GREECE
THE ART OF THE NORTH AMERICAN INDIAN
THE ART OF THE ESKIMO

•

Ancient Rome began as a tiny country village about twenty-seven hundred years ago. The village grew, took over neighboring towns, then all of Italy. Finally Rome conquered most of the known world and became an empire. France, Spain, Greece, Israel, Syria, Egypt, and parts of Britain and Germany are among the lands that were once ruled by the Roman Empire.

The Romans admired the art that they found in some of these lands and brought back art treasures and foreign artists. The Romans developed their own architecture, sculpture, and painting based on the art of other lands.

About fifteen hundred years ago the empire was conquered by invaders from the north and east. Today Rome, no longer the center of a powerful empire, is the capital city of modern Italy.

One of the wonders of ancient Rome
is Trajan's Column. It is a marble pillar 125 feet high,
covered by 2,500 carved figures.
It was put up in A.D. 113 and is still standing
among the ruins of ancient buildings.

The column honors Trajan, a Roman emperor,
who won many battles. It tells the story of his victories,
starting at the bottom of the pillar
and winding upward to the top.
The story is carved in relief. A relief is a raised picture
that stands out from the background.

At the right is a detail, or part, of the column.
Soldiers on horseback are crossing a river
and attacking a walled city.

Once a statue of Trajan stood on top of the column.
Now one of St. Peter stands in its place.

The ancient Romans came to love Greek art after they conquered Greece and her colonies. They made copies of Greek statues and paintings. The crowned figure of a woman is a Roman copy of a Greek statue. She represents the city of Antioch. She is sitting on a rock and is resting one foot on a swimming boy, who stands for the river flowing alongside the city.

Ancient Roman artists are famous for portrait sculpture. Portraits are likenesses of real people. On the right is a portrait of Julius Caesar, one of the most famous generals and rulers of all time. The sculptor even carved the wrinkles in Caesar's forehead.

Roman families honored their ancestors. Their portraits, made of wax or stone, were displayed in an important place in the Roman home. Later, families also displayed portraits of living persons. On the right is a portrait of a great lady of ancient Rome. Her large eyes are gentle, and the smoothness of the marble makes her skin seem soft. The hairdress of piled-up curls was the fashion at the end of the first century A.D.

Capitoline Museum, Rome   Photograph, German Archaeological Institute, Rome

Augustus was the first Roman emperor. During his time Roman writers, painters, sculptors, and builders did some of their best work. This is a larger than life-size marble statue of Augustus. He stands as a victorious general, talking to his troops. He is wearing armor beautifully decorated with figures in relief. The figures stand for the gods of the sky and earth and for the emperor's military victories. At the emperor's feet a baby rides on a dolphin. The child probably represents a cupid, to connect Augustus with the goddess Venus, mother of Cupid.

Marcus Aurelius was another great Roman emperor. His statue stands in the center of a square in the city of Rome. The emperor looks proud and kingly as he sits on his horse. He rides without saddle or stirrups. In his time they were not yet used by the Romans.

The statue was once painted gold, and there are still traces of gold paint on the emperor's face and cape and on the head of the lively horse.

Michelangelo, the great sixteenth century artist, designed the new base that the statue now stands on.

Roman emperors liked to have their portraits on coins, to make themselves known throughout the empire. The face on this coin is a portrait of Marcus Aurelius.

Courtesy British Museum

A mosaic is a decoration made of tiny pieces of colored stones set closely together. The Romans often made their floors of mosaic.

These two pictures are parts of a large Roman mosaic, made from about one and a half million tiny stones. It was a copy of a Greek painting made two hundred years before. The Greek painting is lost.

Roman copies, like this one, show what lost Greek paintings looked like.

The mosaic shows Alexander the Great at the moment of victory over Darius, king of the Persians. In the section above, Alexander charges bravely with his spear. In the section on the right Darius retreats, fleeing in his chariot. The mosaic seems to jump with the excitement of the battle.

National M
Alinari-Art Re

The Roman Empire stretched as far as sunny Egypt. Soldiers and travelers returned with memories of strange birds and beasts. This mosaic, filled with animals that lived in the great Nile River of Egypt, decorated the floor of a Roman house.

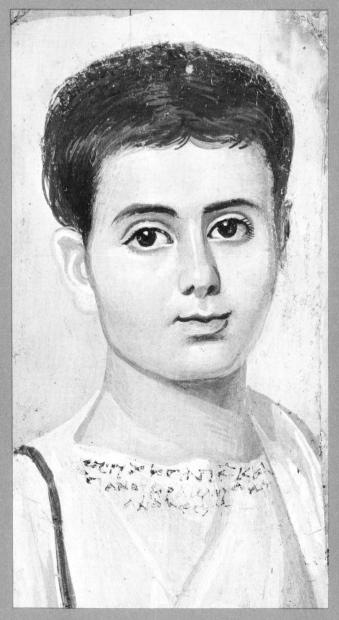

This portrait of a handsome, dark-eyed boy was painted about eighteen hundred years ago when the Romans ruled Egypt. It was an Egyptian custom to put a portrait of the dead person on his mummy case. The artist mixed his colors with hot wax, which made the paint thick and creamy. The portrait looks fresh and alive, as if it had been done today.

ΔΙΟΣΚΟΥΡΙΔΗΣ ΣΑΜΙΟΣ ΕΠΟΙΗΣΕ

Museum of Fine Arts, Boston
Photograph by Alfred H. Tamarin

The gay mosaic on the left, copied from a Greek painting, shows an ancient street scene. The actors are dancing to the rhythm of a double flute, finger cymbals, and a hand drum. All three are wearing masks. The artist even shows the folds of their clothing in the tiny colored stones of the mosaic.

Above is another mosaic, of a donkey nursing two lion cubs. Stones of many colors were used to get light and dark shades in the picture.

The Romans liked to watch chariot races. They were held in large arenas called circuses. The most famous of the racing arenas was the Circus Maximus.

There were usually four drivers in a race. Each wore a costume of a different color—white, red, green, and blue. The driver stood in his chariot and wrapped the reins around his body.

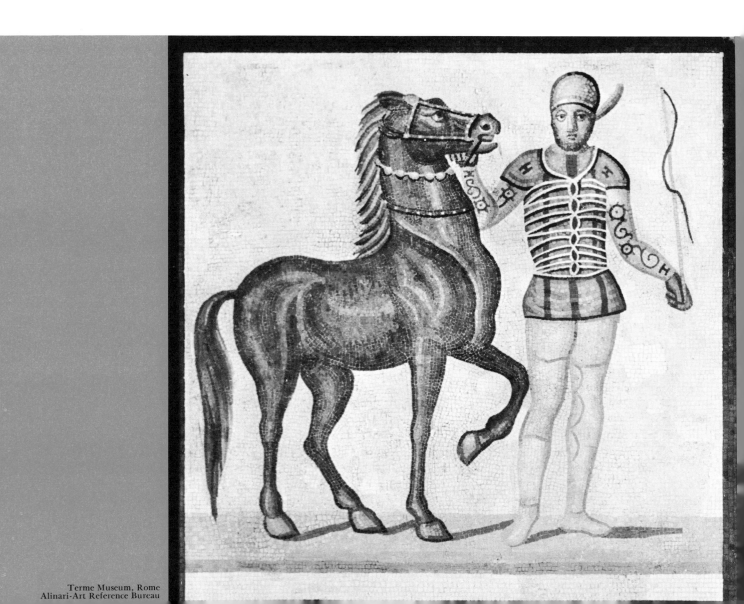

The mosaic on the left shows a charioteer leading his horse. His leg guards and round cap are for protection in case of an accident.

In this marble relief a Roman charioteer is driving his four horses around the racecourse. The cone-shaped pillars are markers, and the chariot will turn around them. Roman chariots had two wheels and were pulled by either two or four horses.

Lateran Museum, Rome
Alinari-Art Reference Bureau

The Romans also enjoyed watching trained fighters, called gladiators, fighting one another to the death. These gladiators were often the toughest prisoners of war captured by the Roman armies. The bronze helmet above, decorated with fine relief carvings, was worn by a gladiator. The reliefs show scenes from the fall of Troy.

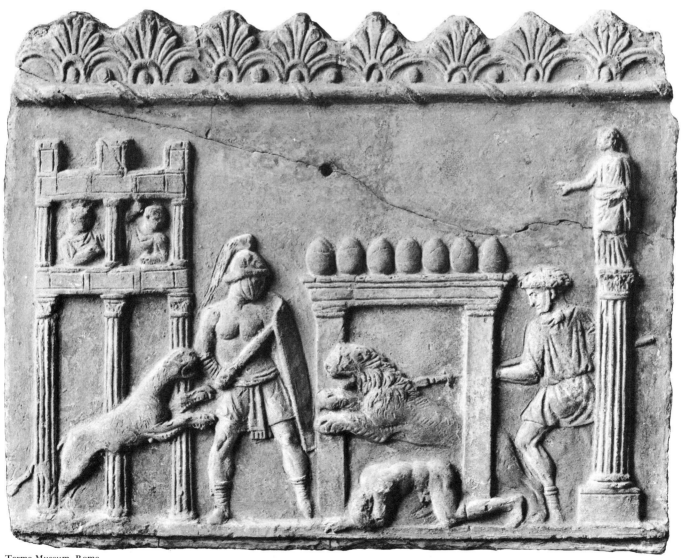

Gladiators also fought wild beasts. The performances were held in round or oval buildings called amphitheaters. The Colosseum, shown on the coin above, was the largest. It held about fifty thousand people. The huge building can still be seen in Rome, although it is partly in ruins.

Fototeca Unione, Rome

The Pantheon is the best-preserved building from ancient Rome. It was built in the time of the emperor Hadrian, around A.D. 125.

The Pantheon is famous for its round design. Everything is round except the porch in front, with the row of columns.

The huge ceiling on the left is a dome. A dome is like the inside of a cup set upside down. The dome of the Pantheon looks like an indoor sky. A round hole at the center of the dome lets in the only light.

Romans were master builders, and the Pantheon is a marvel of building design. The widest distance across the building is exactly the same as the distance from the floor to the top of the dome. The height of the walls is the same as the height of the dome. The walls of the Pantheon are twenty feet thick, to support the weight of the dome.

The Pantheon was built as a temple to the Roman gods. In A.D. 608 it became a Christian church. In later times it was used as the burial place of great men. The painter Raphael is buried there.

Photograph by G. E.

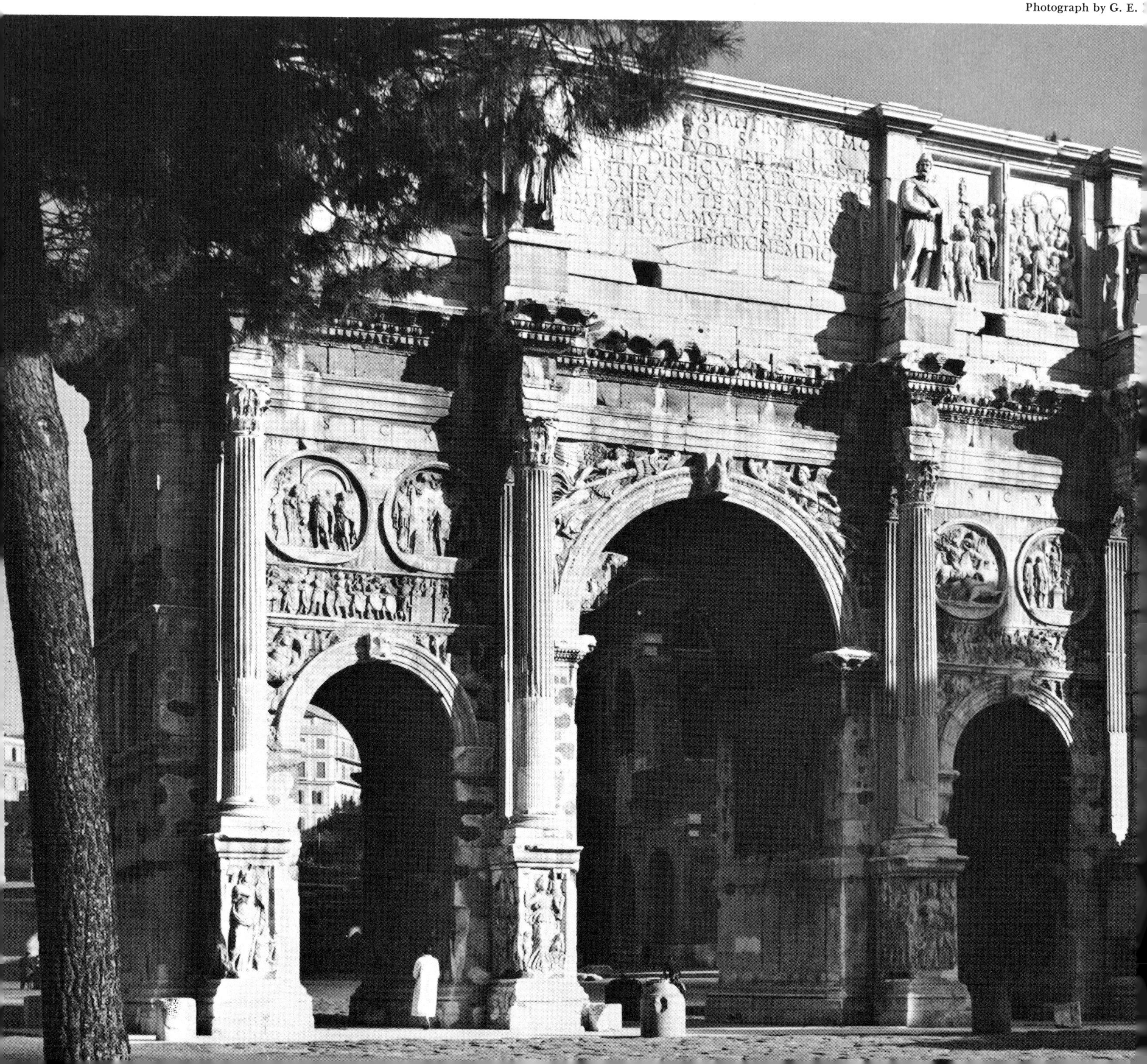

The Romans were the first to build the special type of monument called the Arch of Triumph, to celebrate winning a war. Several arches of triumph still stand in Rome. On the left is the Arch of the emperor Constantine. It was built around A.D. 315, but some of the reliefs and statues were taken from earlier monuments.

On the right is part of a relief from the Arch of the emperor Titus. It was built to mark the victory of Titus in the Judean War. The war ended in the destruction of the Temple in Jerusalem, in A.D. 70.

The relief shows Roman soldiers in a procession, or parade, through Rome. They are carrying the Menorah, or sacred seven-branched candlestick, from the Temple.

Pompeii was a lovely town on the shores of the Mediterranean Sea. Many wealthy Romans built beautiful villas, or country houses, near Pompeii. They filled their villas with statues and covered the walls with murals, or wall paintings. The houses in the town were also filled with art.

Mount Vesuvius, a volcano near Pompeii, erupted in A.D. 79 and buried the town under sixty feet of volcanic ashes. It remained covered and preserved for seventeen hundred years.

Favorite subjects in the mural paintings were pictures of the gods and portraits of real people, animals, and children. On the left a winged cupid drives a chariot pulled by a pair of playful dolphins.

Above is a detail of another Pompeian mural. A gentle, thoughtful girl is holding a writing tool called a stylus. She is thinking of what to write on the tablet in her hand.

On the left is one of the most beautiful paintings from ancient times. It shows a lady playing a musical instrument called a cithara. A young girl, perhaps her daughter, looks out from behind the chair. They were painted with great skill. The lights and shadows make the figures look almost as solid as statues.

The mural below shows Roman children worshiping the goddess Diana. The group on the left, holding torches, are singing to the goddess. The rest of the children are forming a parade in Diana's honor.

Bardo Museum, Tunis

The Romans believed in many gods who looked and acted like people. On the left is a mural with Venus, goddess of love and beauty, seated on a rock. She has just punished her young son Cupid, who is being led away.

Above is a mosaic showing Diana as goddess of the hunt, taking aim with her bow and arrow. Diana was also goddess of the moon. She guided her silvery chariot through the sky at night.

National Museum, Naples
Alinari-Art Reference Bureau

The heroes of Homer's *Iliad* and *Odyssey* were also popular in Roman art. On the left is a detail of a large painting. It shows Achilles, hero of the Greek war against Troy, told about in the *Iliad*.

The mosaic above is a scene from the *Odyssey*. It tells a story about the Greek hero Odysseus, whose Roman name was Ulysses. He had his sailors tie him to the mast of his ship so he could sail safely past the island of the Sirens and still hear their music. The Sirens were part woman, part bird. Their songs were so sweet that sailors went searching for them and wrecked their ships on the rocks. Ulysses put wax into the ears of his sailors so they could not hear the Sirens' music.

Bardo Museum, Tunis

The farmlands in North Africa were important to the empire. Wheat, olive oil, and wine were shipped across the Mediterranean Sea to Europe.

This mosaic shows a charming Roman country house in North Africa, with ducks and birds wandering about.

Photograph by Richard E. Morley

Louvre, Paris
Alinari-Art Reference Bureau

Leptis Magna, a rich city on the African coast of the Mediterranean Sea, had some fine public buildings. This head of a Gorgon, a creature from mythology, is on a wall that still stands in Leptis Magna. A Gorgon is a monster with snakes for hair. Anyone looking at her would turn to stone instantly. There is a myth that the Greek hero Perseus cut off the head of a Gorgon named Medusa. He used his shield as a mirror so that he would not have to look directly at her. The silver plate on the left is decorated with a crowned woman holding a horn of plenty, which stands for the rich harvests in North Africa.

This is the Gemma Augustea, a cameo carving. It is carved in sardonyx, a beautiful stone with layers of white and yellow-orange. In the upper part Augustus is being crowned with a wreath of oak leaves. Below, soldiers are putting up a trophy.

Kunsthistorisches Museum, Vienna

Louvre, Paris
Photograph Giraudon

Above is a cameo with a figure of an eagle, the emblem of the Roman Empire. A model of an eagle mounted on a pole was carried at the head of Roman armies when they went into battle.

The bronze rooster on the right shows the Roman love for the countryside with its farm animals. The rooster is complete down to its smallest feather. It looks as if it is going to crow.

Children had an important place in
Roman art. Statues were made of the children
and grandchildren of the emperor.
At the left is the head of a bronze statue,
thought to be a prince
of the House of Augustus.

At the right, above, is a relief
showing a scene in a Roman school.
Two children are reading from scrolls.
A child who came in late
is greeting the teacher.

In the relief below, a father tenderly
holds his infant son as a young boy
drives a chariot pulled by a goat.
The scene is a detail from a larger relief
showing four stages
in the education of a Roman boy.

Wherever their armies went, Roman art can be found today, even in places as far from Rome as England and Africa.

Now Rome is a modern city, but many ancient buildings, statues, and fountains still stand. The old and the new are side by side in modern Rome.

40

Statue of Silenus
Conservatori Museum, Rome

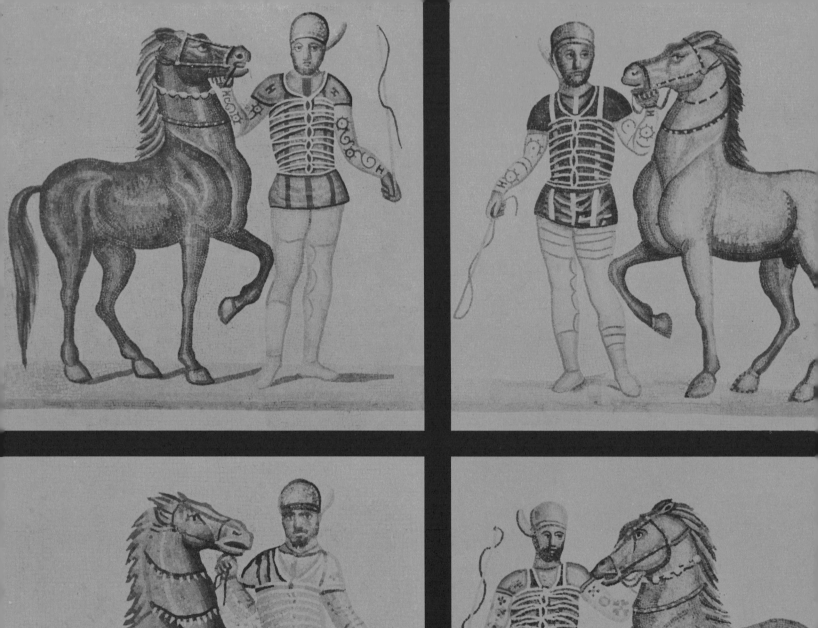

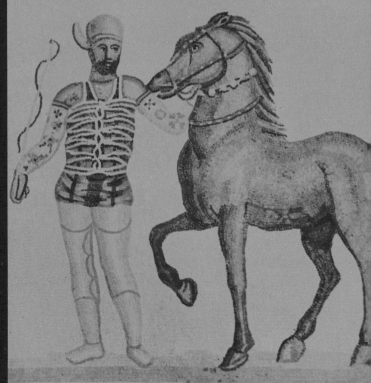

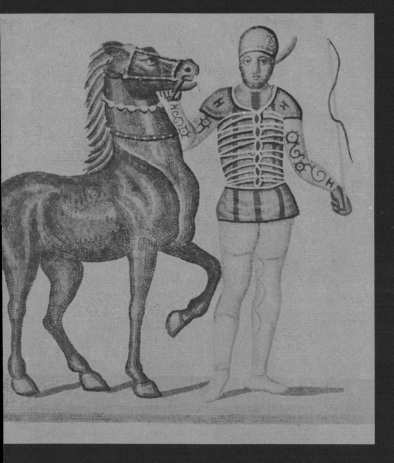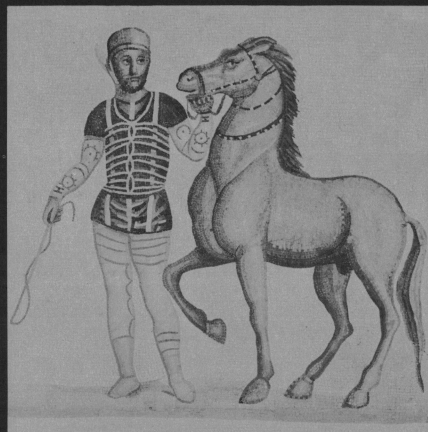
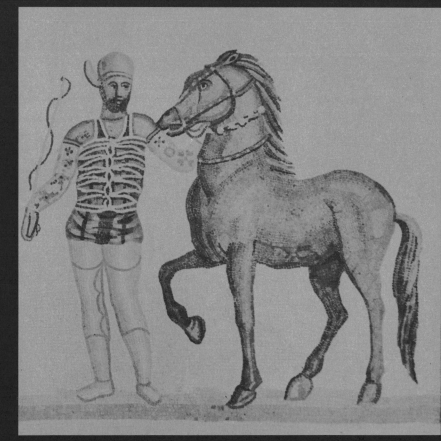

7 5